# Food and Recipes of the Thirteen Colonies

George Erdosh

The Rosen Publishing Group's
**PowerKids Press™**
New York

The recipes in this cookbook are intended for a child to make together with an adult.

*Many thanks to Ruth Rosen and her test kitchen.*

Published in 1997 by The Rosen Publishing Group, Inc.
29 East 21st Street, New York, NY 10010

First Edition

Book Design: Danielle Primiceri

Photo Credits: Cover (left) © Corbis-Bettmann, (right) © Steven Ferry/P & F Communictions, pp. 4, 7, 8, 10 (bottom, bottom right), 12 (top), 16 (top, middle) © Corbis-Bettmann; p. 12 © PhotoDisc; p. 14 © Bettmann; 18 (top) © Joe Viesti/Viesti Associates, Inc.; p. 18 (middle) © Artville, LLC; p. 20 (top) © Ofori Akyea; p. 20 (middle) Sheldon Hine/Archive Photos.

Photo Illustrations: pp. 10 (top, middle), 12 (middle, bottom), 16 (middle, bottom), 18 (middle, bottom), 20 (middle, bottom) by Ira Fox; pp. 11, 13, 17, 19, 21 by Christine Innamorato and Olga Vega.

Erdosh, George, 1935–
    Food and recipes of the thirteen colonies / George Erdosh.
    Includes index.
    Summary: Describes some of the foods prepared in the various areas of what would become the United States during the colonial period. Includes recipes.
    ISBN 0-8239-5114-6
    1. Cookery, American—History—Juvenile literature. 2. United States—History—Colonial period, ca. 1600–1775—Juvenile literature. 3. Food habits—United States—History—17th century—Juvenile literature. 4. Food habits—United States—History—18th century—Juvenile literature. [1. Cookery, American—History. 2. United States—History—Colonial period, ca. 1600–1775.]
    TX715.E665 1997
    641.5973'09032—dc21                                                      97-29812
                                                                                CIP
                                                                                AC

Manufactured in the United States of America

# Contents

# Sarah Learns to Cook

Sarah walked through the snow to her neighbor's house in the darkness of the early morning. Her mother was out of maple syrup for breakfast so she sent Sarah to borrow some. As she walked, she thought about the breakfast pudding that her mother would make that morning. Maybe her mother would let her put some dried cranberries in it. Sarah and her brother spent hours picking cranberries last fall. Sarah helped her mother dry them so they could store the berries for the winter. Sarah couldn't wait to get back home. She was hungry for a good **colonial** (kul-OH-nee-ul) breakfast.

◀ *Colonial cooks rose early in the morning to cook big breakfasts for their families.*

# What Were the Thirteen Colonies?

The thirteen **colonies** (KOL-un-eez) were the beginning of what would later become the United States. Groups of people sailed from England to North America in the mid-1600s. They wanted to make new lives for themselves. They **settled** (SET-tuld) along the East Coast of North America in areas that were called colonies. Once settled, these people were called **colonists** (KOL-un-ists). The colonies were under British rule, but people came from all over Europe to settle there.

The northern colonies were called New England. They included Massachusetts, New Hampshire, Connecticut, and Rhode Island. The middle colonies, which were along the middle of the East Coast, were New York, New Jersey, Pennsylvania, and Delaware. The southern colonies included North Carolina, South Carolina, Georgia, Virginia, and Maryland.

*The Pilgrims sailed from England to North America in 1620. They settled in what is now Plymouth, Massachusetts.* ▶

The Thirteen Colonies

# New Foods

Although the colonists were making new lives, they didn't like change very much. They wanted to be able to live the same way and eat the same foods they ate in England and Europe. But many of these foods did not grow in America. And most of the seeds the colonists brought with them did not grow well.

The colonists learned to cook and eat new foods. They learned to farm, hunt, and fish from the Native Americans who had lived on the land for hundreds of years. By the year 1700, the colonists had big farms and lots of food. Their meals were a mix of **traditional** (truh-DISH-un-ul) English food, such as meat, cheese, and butter, and Native American food, such as corn, beans, and pumpkins.

◀ *The colonists learned from the Native Americans new ways to raise crops. This helped the colonists to grow more crops than they had been able to grow on the same amount of land in England.*

# Cooking Over the Fire

Cooking was a lot different during colonial times than it is now. Women did all the cooking. They did not have stoves, ovens, or **refrigerators** (ree-FRIJ-er-ay-terz) like we do today. They cooked in big kettles over an open fire. Most meals were stews made of meat, corn, turnips, and other vegetables. A heavy, brown bread was cooked in the steam that rose from the stew.

For breakfast, many people in New England ate **hasty** (HAY-stee) pudding. It was called hasty pudding because it was quick and easy to make. Colonists could make it with "haste."

# Hasty Pudding

1 cup cornmeal
½ teaspoon salt
4 cups water
maple syrup
milk or half-and-half

## Safety Tip

Watch out for hot splashing water!

## HOW TO DO IT:

☞ Mix one cup of water with the cornmeal in a small bowl.

☞ Boil the other 3 cups of water with the salt in a medium-sized pot.

☞ When the water boils, turn the heat down to low and slowly stir in the cornmeal mixture. Stir until the cornmeal is thick, about three to five minutes.

☞ Turn off the stove, put the lid on the pot, and let it sit for three minutes.

☞ Stir the pudding again and serve it.

☞ Serve with maple syrup or half-and-half. If you like, add ½ cup raisins to the cornmeal before cooking it.

This serves four people.

# New Foods, New Recipes

Many foods that did not grow in the colonies, such as sugar, were shipped there from England. But these things cost too much to use every day. Instead of sugar, most colonists cooked with **molasses** (moh-LAS-ez) and maple syrup. Molasses also came from English sugar factories, but it was cheaper than sugar. Most colonists made maple syrup from the sap drained from maple trees that grew on their land.

Colonial cooks had no cookbooks. Women passed on their **recipes** (RESS-ih-peez) by teaching them to their daughters. The first American cookbook was published in 1742. One popular recipe at that time was for flat jacks, which are like pancakes.

# Flat Jacks

1 cup cornmeal

½ cup all-purpose flour

½ teaspoon salt

½ teaspoon baking soda*

¼ teaspoon powdered ginger

2 tablespoons butter

1½ teaspoons molasses

1½ cups buttermilk

¼ cup vegetable oil

## Safety Tip

Ask your adult helper to help you fry these.

## HOW TO DO IT:

☞ Sift the cornmeal, flour, salt, baking powder, and ginger into a medium-sized bowl.

☞ Melt the butter on very low heat in a small pan. Pour it into another bowl and mix it with the molasses and buttermilk.

☞ Stir the liquid mixture into the dry ingredients. Mix until just combined.

☞ Heat oil in a frying pan.

☞ Fry about ½ cup of batter in hot oil.

☞ Serve with honey or maple syrup.

This serves three people.

*Baking soda makes the flat jacks rise up a little. The Native Americans used wood ash to do the same thing.

13

# Food of the New England Colonies

It was hard for farmers in the New England colonies to grow enough fruits and vegetables to feed their families. The soil was not very good, and the growing season was too short. So the colonists ate a lot of meat and fish. They hunted animals in the forests and fished in the ocean.

Colonists in New England rarely ate fresh vegetables. And they never ate salads. They cooked their vegetables into sauces that they ate with meat.

After a few years, boats brought goats and cows from England. Then the New England colonists also had fresh milk, butter, and cheeses to eat.

◀ *Most colonists relied on hunting and fishing for food.*

# Food of the Middle Colonies

The growing season in the middle colonies was longer and the soil was better than in the New England colonies. There were Dutch and German settlers in these colonies. They brought their own food traditions with them. The Dutch brought cheeses, cookies, cakes, and pastries. The Germans brought cabbage, rye bread, and different ways to cook pork.

Colonial cooks baked often. At first, bread was cooked over the fire. Then brick ovens were built into the inside walls of fireplaces. Later, the ovens were moved outside of the fireplaces. And finally, cast-iron stoves became popular. Women baked breads, pies, cakes, cookies, and other pastries about once a week.

# Dutch Walnut-Cinnamon Squares

8 ounces (1 cup) butter, softened

1 cup sugar

1 egg—the egg yolk in one bowl, the egg white in another

2 cups all-purpose flour

1 teaspoon salt

1½ tablespoons cinnamon

1½ cups chopped walnuts

## HOW TO DO IT:

☞ Preheat the oven to 325° F. Grease a 9 x 13-inch baking pan with butter or shortening.

☞ Cream butter and sugar with a mixer on medium speed for two minutes. Stir in egg yolk.

☞ Sift flour, salt, and cinnamon into a bowl. Add the mixture to the butter mixture one spoonful at a time, mixing at a low speed until dough is formed.

☞ Scrape the dough into the pan. Press the dough evenly into the pan.

☞ Beat the egg white in a small bowl with a fork until foamy. Pour it over the dough and spread. Sprinkle the nuts evenly on the dough.

☞ Bake for 20 to 25 minutes.

☞ When the pastry is cool, ask your adult helper to help you cut it into squares.

This serves six people.

# Food of the South

The colonists in the South had a good **climate** (KLY-met) for growing crops. They also had a long growing season. They could grow many kinds of foods. And, like the colonists in New England, they ate a lot of meat. But because the weather was so warm, food spoiled quickly. Southern cooks hid the bad **flavor** (FLAY-ver) by adding spices, such as black pepper and chili pepper.

Corn was one food that grew well in all of the colonies. Native Americans taught the colonists how to make corn even more **nutritious** (new-TRISH-us) by removing the **hulls** (HULZ) from the **kernels** (KER-nulz). They called this corn **hominy** (HAH-men-ee). Hominy was often eaten with vegetables and meats.

# Southern Succotash

## You will need:

2 cups frozen lima beans*

2 cups frozen hominy or white corn*

1 tablespoon butter

½ teaspoon sugar

½ teaspoon salt

¼ teaspoon ground black pepper

¼ cup heavy cream

## HOW TO DO IT:

☞ Cook the lima beans in boiling water in a medium-size pot until nearly soft, then drain them.

☞ Put the lima beans back in the pot. Add the frozen corn, butter, sugar, salt, and black pepper. Turn the heat to medium and put the uncovered pot on the stove. Cook for 10 minutes, stirring every few minutes.

☞ Turn the heat to low. Stir in the cream, cook for five more minutes, then serve.

This serves four to five people.

* There were no frozen foods in the colonies. But to make succotash easier to make, we will use frozen vegetables.

# Food from Africa

Many southern farmers had **slaves** (SLAYVZ). Slaves were people who were brought from Africa to North America against their will to work on farms. Slaves were "owned" by their masters. They were forced to work long hours with little rest. They were not paid for their work. Slaves had no freedom and no rights until 1865, when slavery was outlawed.

Although slaves did not choose to come to the United States, they added a lot to American food and cooking traditions. Many slaves brought seeds of African plants, such as black-eyed peas, okra, and peanuts, with them to plant in the new country. They also brought different ways of cooking. Their food was more spicy than English or Native American food.

# Hoppin' John

2 cups frozen black-eyed peas

1 medium chopped onion

½ teaspoon salt

½ teaspoon ground black pepper

¼ teaspoon ground chili

1 clove garlic, minced

1 bay leaf

8 ounces bacon

## HOW TO DO IT:

☞ Add the frozen black-eyed peas and one cup of water to a medium-sized pot. Turn the heat to medium and put the pot on the stove.

☞ While the peas are cooking, add the onion, salt, black pepper, chili, garlic, bay leaf, and uncooked bacon.

☞ When the water boils, turn heat down to low, cover the pot, and simmer for one hour.

☞ Stir from time to time. Check to make sure there is some water left in the pot. If it is dry, add two tablespoons of water.

☞ Serve hoppin' john with hot, white rice.

This serves two to three people.

# Traditions from the Colonies

The early traditional food of the colonies came first from England and the Native Americans, then from Holland and Germany, and later from Africa. These food traditions blended together to become American food.

This still happens today. Every time a new group of people moves to the United States, they bring their food, spices, and ways of cooking with them. Slowly, other people blend these with their own foods and methods of cooking. In this way, American food and cooking continues to grow and change.

# Glossary

**climate** (KLY-met)  The weather of a place throughout the year.

**colonial** (kul-OH-nee-ul)  A way to describe anything that has to do with the colonists or the colonies.

**colonist** (KOL-un-ist)  A person who moves from his own country to a new land, but stays under the rule of the old country.

**colony** (KOL-un-ee)  Area of land settled by people from another country and under the rule of the old country.

**flavor** (FLAY-ver)  The way something tastes.

**hasty** (HAY-stee)  Quick or speedy.

**hominy** (HAH-men-ee)  Corn that has the hulls removed and is white in color.

**hull** (HUL)  The very tip of a kernel or seed.

**kernel** (KER-nul)  A seed of corn.

**molasses** (moh-LAS-ez)  The thick, sweet liquid that is left over when cane sugar is turned into white sugar.

**nutritious** (new-TRISH-us)  A way to describe food that is healthy and good for the body.

**recipe** (RESS-ih-pee)  Directions to cook a food.

**settle** (SET-tul)  To set up house in a new land.

**refrigerator** (ree-FRIJ-er-ay-ter)  A machine that keeps food cold.

**slave** (SLAYV)  A person who is "owned" by another person.

**traditional** (truh-DISH-un-ul)  A belief or practice that is handed down from parent to child.

# Index

## DATE DUE

| | | | |
|---|---|---|---|
| FEB 2 8 '00 | | | |
| JUL 0 9 '00 | | | |
| JUN 1 4 '00 | ILL# 9464429 CTB | | |
| MAY 1 3 2003 | | | |
| JAN 0 3 2011 | | | |
| | | | |
| | | | |
| | | | |
| | | | |
| | | | |
| | | | |
| | | | |
| | | | |
| | | | |
| | | | |
| | | | |
| | | | |
| | | | |
| GAYLORD | | | PRINTED IN U.S.A. |